T0299604

The Simple Guide to Attachment Difficulties in Children

also in the Simple Guides *series*

The Simple Guide to Child Trauma
What It Is and How to Help
Betsy de Thierry
Illustrated by Emma Reeves
Foreword by David Shemmings
ISBN 978 1 78592 136 0
eISBN 978 1 78450 401 4

The Simple Guide to Sensitive Boys
How to Nurture Children and Avoid Trauma
Betsy de Thierry
Illustrated by Emma Reeves
Foreword by Jane Evans
ISBN 978 1 78592 325 8
eISBN 978 1 78450 639 1

The Simple Guide to Understanding Shame in Children
What It Is, What Helps and How to Prevent Further Stress or Trauma
Betsy de Thierry
Illustrated by Emma Reeves
Foreword by Dr Marc Bush
ISBN 978 1 78592 505 4
eISBN 978 1 78450 895 1

The Simple Guide to Complex Trauma and Dissociation
What It Is and How to Help
Betsy de Thierry
Illustrated by Emma Reeves
Foreword by Graham Music
ISBN 978 1 78775 314 3
eISBN 978 1 78775 315 0

The Simple Guide to Collective Trauma
What It Is, How It Affects Us and How to Help
Betsy de Thierry
Illustrated by Emma Reeves
Foreword by Lisa Cherry
ISBN 978 1 78775 788 2
eISBN 978 1 78775 789 9

The
Simple Guide to Attachment Difficulties in Children

What They Are and How to Help

Betsy de Thierry

Foreword by Carrie Grant

Illustrated by Emma Reeves

Jessica Kingsley Publishers

London and Philadelphia

This book is dedicated to my sons,
Joshua, Benjamin, Jonah and Noah.

First published in 2019
by Jessica Kingsley Publishers
73 Collier Street
London N1 9BE, UK
and
400 Market Street, Suite 400
Philadelphia, PA 19106, USA

www.jkp.com

Copyright © Betsy de Thierry 2019
Foreword copyright © Carrie Grant 2019
Illustrations copyright © Emma Reeves 2019

Library of Congress Cataloging in Publication Data
A CIP catalog record for this book is available from the Library of Congress

British Library Cataloguing in Publication Data
A CIP catalogue record for this book is available from the British Library

ISBN 978 1 78592 639 6
eISBN 978 1 78592 640 2

Printed and bound in Great Britain

CONTENTS

FOREWORD

The relationship between parent and child is the most profound of all: in birth, the symbolism of the umbilical cord attaching the supplier to the supplied, the bearer to the born; this other, that is so physiologically close and yet sadly, has the potential to become emotionally, mentally and spiritually disconnected.

As a mum to four children – three birth children and one adopted child – I have been able to observe different styles of attachment at very close quarters. All our children have special needs, including two autistic girls, and the way in which these incredible children have attached with us and we to them has been a wonderful journey to embark upon. When David and I adopted our son, we thought we had a real advantage with any attachment issues that might arise, as we were already 'genned-up' parents. As vocal coaches, we were attuned to truly hearing people whatever they were saying; we were full of strategies and confident that our love in action could bring this little boy round to a place of feeling safe, held, contained, secure and, most importantly, loved.

What we hadn't accounted for was that it takes two to attach, and we soon found our best efforts were not enough. Hand on heart, I can honestly say I love all my children equally, but restoring attachment demands more than love.

When our son was adopted in 2011, he instantly attached to my husband, David. Our adoption training taught us that adopted children sometimes get to a point where they simply cannot attach any more, so I was overjoyed at our son's ability to connect. Two years into my parenting journey, I was still failing with my son; I felt rejected, and my own inner abandoned child began to surface. I tried harder, but my best efforts were met with silence, defiance and even violence.

And so we started on the long road of discovering about trauma and its effects. We had to learn what we were dealing with. We discovered that the shattering of a child's trust cannot be papered over with a few months or even years of committed, loving parenting. David and I had to get ourselves healed up and tooled up for the battle ahead. What we needed at this point was insight and revelation.

We are now a few years further down the road, and the attachment is definitely there; it's secure, and at root level it is permanent. The day-to-day workings can be challenging, but we now have a solid base to work from. My little boy and I are attached.

This easy-to-read book provides the kind of help we were looking for; it lays the problem out clearly and then seeks to offer insight and not trite solutions. Betsy also has a way of making the parent feel as if they can actually get this stuff right. There is no blame and shame, only observation and inspiration.

The reflection points at the end of each chapter are really helpful for conversation and planning. This book could also be used in groups to train and support one another. How I wish we had had this book to study before we adopted.

Carrie Grant

INTRODUCTION

Attachment is such an important subject because living a full life has to involve relationships. We are born totally dependent on relationships for survival and spend the majority of our life working and living alongside others. Whilst relationships can cause huge pain and turmoil, they are also important to really feel alive.

This book is a simple guide to attachment. As in my previous books, I feel immense pressure to draw attention to so many theorists and experts in this field who have spent years researching and developing theories and yet I have to resign myself to knowing that I can only mention some and explore them less than I'd really want to. I hope you'll understand that the aim and intention of this book is to give an overview, to help those who are unable to study the rich literature out there in depth. It's an overview that I hope people can apply to their homes and workplaces immediately with ease. I am sorry if I haven't covered all that you needed me to; it was difficult to keep this 'short' and 'simple'. I do feel that this book needs to be accompanied with *The Simple Guide to Child Trauma* (2016) and *The Simple Guide to Understanding Shame in Children* (2018), and together the three books combined will enable a more thorough understanding.

As with all my books in this series, the majority of the content is still applicable to people of any age despite the focus on children. Ultimately, no matter what age we are, when we have been hurt in a relationship, real healing has to come from a relationship. The older we get, the more complex and multi layered our coping mechanisms can become and so the longer it can take to unpick and unpack those in order to rewire our brains to heal. But healing is very possible, and comes in a similar way – through relationships, self-awareness and processing negative experiences.

I do hope that the book helps you as you seek to change lives by offering relationships that are consistent, kind, nurturing, empathetic and emotionally available.

Let's be committed to building communities where there is no shame or blame, but instead support, emotional connection, empathy and kindness.

Well done for all that you are doing! Thank you on behalf of the children that you are reading about… keep going and one day they may well write to say how much you impacted their lives.

Betsy

Chapter One

WHAT IS ATTACHMENT?

Attachment is a word that is used to describe the ability to enable a child to feel emotionally and physically safe through their relationship with their 'main adult(s)' who care for them. Attachment theory was first developed by a psychologist called John Bowlby (1988), who was fascinated by the early relationship between babies and their mother and how much that affected them as they grew up. The concept has developed from being solely about a mother and her baby to cover the whole experience of a child's ability to feel intrinsically emotionally safe with their primary carer(s).

My assumption is that you are reading this book because you care about a child and want the best for them. It could be that you are a birth parent who has experienced trauma and you recognise that your child(ren) have been affected by that difficult time and you want to be able to see them recover and heal. Maybe you are an adoptive parent who is focused on developing a positive and healing relationship with your child(ren). You could be a foster parent or teacher or Teaching Assistant (TA) who is working with children who need you to help them heal from past difficult relational experiences. Maybe you are a youth worker, parenting worker or another member of the workforce who is focused on helping children and young people heal from difficult experiences that have caused them to behave in ways that are challenging.

In the children's workforce the word attachment is becoming used frequently and so the exact definition is important as we explore the concept in this little book. I have offered my definition and here are those of some other professionals:

> Attachment is one specific aspect of the relationship between a child and a parent with its purpose being to make a child safe, secure and protected. (Benoit 2018)

> An attachment is a precise term: the notion of a safe haven, which, when available, becomes a secure base from which to explore the world around us. Then when we are separated from our secure base we become anxious and quickly seek proximity. (Shemmings 2016a)

> In infancy and childhood, attachment figures both provide protection and also teach children how to make meaning of the information available to their minds. (Crittenden 2005)

I would assert that attachment is the specific element of parenting that goes beyond the physical needs of the child being met and speaks of the emotional availability of the child's primary caregiver to be an emotional safety regulator for the child. This book will explore the challenges of this role and also look at ways to repair difficult attachment experiences.

How does a healthy attachment develop?

Healthy attachment relationship develops from before birth as the mother responds to the baby's movements and interacts with the unborn baby with words, sounds and touch that demonstrate love and nurture. Evidence now suggests that the baby responds to this in the womb and when they are born they recognise the familiar voices. Research by Sullivan and colleagues shows a specific developmental period when this begins:

> This attachment begins during the last trimester of pregnancy, when auditory and olfactory systems become functional, allowing the fetus to learn about the mother's voice and odours. (2011)

From birth the parent responds to the then explicit needs of the child. Whilst there is a natural recognition of the vulnerability of the baby that causes most people older than the baby to respond with a strong protective reaction, attachment is a specific response that:

- provides safety and security

- regulates emotions by comforting, creating joy, and helping to facilitate calm

- offers a secure base from which to explore 'the world'.

The baby learns to look for the most familiar voice and smell and then responds with relief when they experience the familiarity. The smell and sound become the experience of safety and, as the baby develops, the safety associated with such sensory experiences only strengthens, leading to the child clinging to the legs of the parent, running back to them when they feel nervous or afraid and preferring their company to others.

When the child has had this experience repetitively and consistently they become able to explore 'the world' with the knowledge that their 'safe place' will always be there to return to and feel the familiar sense of relief and comfort. This leads them to be able to develop in confidence that enables them to need the 'safe place' less and less and they grow in identity and internal strength and capacity.

What are the core attachment theories?

Bowlby (1988) and Ainsworth (1978) first explored attachment and asserted the power of this repetitive, consistent, 'safe place' for the baby and child. Bowlby suggests that a significant affectional bond develops between infant and carer known as attachment. He spoke about this bond with the primary caregiver being the 'safe base from which to explore the world'. The safe base is the place that feels like the 'safe haven' to turn to when strong feelings are aroused, which for a baby could be a loud noise, a tummy rumbling or feeling cold; these feelings become more diverse with age.

Ainsworth was interested in the relationship between the mother and baby and what happened when the baby was separated and reunited. Her 'Strange Situation' experiment is a well known pioneering piece of research that explored how the baby responded both when a mother left them on their own and when she left them with a stranger. She concluded that there were different attachment styles and also, just like Bowlby, she came to conclude that a child needed this warm, intimate influence to develop healthy emotions and relationships. They both concluded that during the baby's first year the experiences of being held, noticed, comforted and cared for when frightened are essential to a child's ability to develop in a healthy way. They asserted that the early experiences will affect the development of crucial factors such as the ability to trust in others, self awareness, and the ability to reflect on needs and ask for help. As the child gets older and they can explore their surroundings, they grow up knowing with certainty that there is a safe place to return to and be comforted if their explorations are unsettling or frightening.

Bowlby also asserted that babies form a small hierarchy of attachments where they learn relevant emotional information. This hierarchy helps them to know there is more than one adult to enable safety, so that they can instinctively turn to a familiar face to find comfort. Essentially, early attachment experiences programme a child psychosocially and physiologically.

Internal schemas and internal working model

The theory progresses from being about the impact of the primary caregiver in offering emotional security and safety to believing that the child then forms a semi-permanent relational template from those experiences. This template is used in all further relationships and the child's expectations of other adults. If they had their needs met repetitively then they would have an internal template or schema that caused them to expect other adults to be trustworthy. If they experienced volatility then they would expect other adults to be volatile and they would be more anxious or ambivalent in their relationships. Bowlby described that as an internal working model that can change over time, and even through adulthood, according to relational experiences that are repetitive.

Who can be an attachment figure?

The attachment figure for a baby is usually the adult who is their primary caregiver. This could also be two adults, although one may be a stronger attachment. As the child grows they can have the capacity to find safety and security in other adults and siblings, but these become additional attachment figures rather than replacing the primary caregiver. Attachment theory is continually developing and it has now been evidenced that attachment relationships can be offered by grandparents, aunts, friends, nannies and even older siblings (Howes 1999). Those who offer a long term, nurturing, repetitive, consistent, relationally rewarding experience can become attachment figures if they help the baby or child repetitively navigate their positive and negative feelings in an emotionally warm and available way.

When a child experiences trauma and the primary caregiver is also traumatised, additional attachment figures can help the child feel more secure and safe.

The most important factors to enable a healthy attachment develop are consistency, repetition, and warm, kind, empathetic and patient caregiving.

When it goes wrong

The book will explore in more detail what happens when things go wrong in the area of attachment. First, it's important to recognise that perfect parenting is a concept that doesn't really exist, and that in 1960 the great British psychoanalyst Donald Winnicott created the term 'good enough parenting' to conceptualise the needs for a child to experience consistent availability and predictability from their caring adult but that 'it is normal for fluctuations in the provision of attention and awareness' (de Thierry 2015, p.57). Winnicott states that: 'perfection belongs to machines, and the imperfections that are characteristic of human adaptation to need are an essential quality in the environment that facilitates' (2005, p.187). Attachment-based trauma can occur when a child cannot develop a healthy sense of self or a sense of safety or security with a parent due to their absence, volatility or emotional disengagement. We will look at the coping mechanisms children adopt to survive and how the child can recover from any difficult attachment experiences.

It is worth noting at this stage, however, that this simple guide will not be able to cover the subject in enough depth to facilitate a child with significant attachment difficulties to fully recover; but it will be a good introduction for relatives, friends, teachers and staff to understand why their behaviour can be so dramatically disruptive. We recognise that children with significant attachment trauma can often struggle to live lives free from the crippling burden of complex and severe coping mechanisms which can cause those who are caring for them to become overwhelmed as well. This book will explain why and give an overview of what they need to recover.

Reflection points

- Who are your attachment relationships and how have they impacted you?

- How are you investing into the children in your care and what attachment experience do you think they may have had?

Chapter Two

HOW DOES AN ATTACHMENT DEVELOP AND GET STRONGER?

The essential ability to form attachment is indispensable for human social relationships and we know that it is during repeated interactions with a nurturing and sensitive caregiver that a child is able to develop a secure internal framework that is built on the caregiver's availability for reducing stress and providing comfort in potentially frightening situations.

Children ideally need one or two primary caregivers to help them know that the world is safe and that they are loved. It's literally in the face of this/these adult(s) that they begin to find their own identity. This is because they have the emotional courage and confidence to go and explore 'the world' and who they are, how others respond to them, what they enjoy, what they fear and come back to their safety and security. In babyhood, it's literally in the face of this adult that they feel safe, secure and loved. If children are told that they are loved without the intentional face-to-face interaction, the talking, smiling, looking and laughing, the words have little impact and don't go so deeply into their core sense of self.

In this chapter we'll explore how to develop the attachment relationship. In further chapters we'll look at the repair of attachment breakdown, so don't panic if you read this and know that the child(ren) you are caring for didn't have this positive, nurturing experience due to circumstances that occurred.

The four possible stages of attachment

Schaffer and Emerson (1964) researched 60 babies and their attachment behaviour in Glasgow. Their conclusion was that there are four stages that babies progress through. The first stage is at age 0–6 weeks and here there is no clear discrimination between those around them. They call this the asocial stage. The second stage is from six weeks to six months old and they call this the indiscriminate stage as the babies can tell people apart, have no fear of strangers and yet form attachments with familiar adults. This first specific attachment was formed by 50 per cent of infants between 25 and 32 weeks. From about seven months the babies showed signs of distress about being separated from their primary carer and distress at being with strangers. Around ten months onwards babies develop further attachments and by 18 months 31 per cent had five or more attachments, e.g. to grandparents, etc. There have been many other research projects that evidence very similar stages; these can help us be aware of the natural ways babies develop relationships and their understanding of the world around them.

Essentially the early years are the time when the child learns how to relate to everyone else in their life. Gerhardt describes it like this:

> The most frequent behaviours of the parental figures, both mother and father, will be etched in the baby's neural pathways as guides to relating. These repeated experiences turn into learning, and in terms of the pathways involved in emotion, this consists primarily of learning what to expect from others in close relationship. (2004, p.211)

Although this is strong recognition that early experiences change neural pathways, as a psychotherapist I have the privilege of seeing neural pathways change as other repetitive experiences become dominant and early experiences are processed.

The difference between bonding and attachment

Bonding is a word that was used a lot to describe the early relationship between the baby and mother but is a different concept to attachment. The bonding experience was developed by Klaus and Kennell (1976) and was intrinsically linked with the skin-to-skin contact and the feelings a mother has towards her baby in the early days. Bonding seems to be merely the function of being a close family member whilst attachment speaks of the adult being the emotionally safe place for the child to run to when they are upset or needing reassurance. Therefore, the tricky thing is that the quality of an attachment relationship cannot be evaluated by seeing a child and his dad playing football because there could be anything actually happening in this situation! It could be that the dad is taking on the role of play companion rather than providing the adult emotional safety and security. A healthy attachment cannot therefore be evaluated by seeing the children eating healthy meals, because that could be the parent being in the role as the provider of their physical needs, whereas little attention could be given to the attachment experience of the child. Were they able to feel emotional connection to the parent who was the source of safety and security? A healthy attachment cannot even be measured by seeing a child not wanting to leave their parent and showing anxiety about the separation. In such a situation the child may indeed feel scared about being away from their source of security and safety but equally they may feel scared that their parent is volatile or untrustworthy and may not return or may harm another person that they love. It would be impossible to say which at first glance. So a healthy attachment takes a little more assessment than quick outward displays of a relationship between the child and their parent.

Attunement

Attunement is a way of tuning into the other person and how they are feeling and is an important skill to use when relating to babies, children and others. It's the ability to notice how the person or people around us are feeling or responding and then reacting accordingly. A well attuned person notices the unspoken emotional state of the other person and adapts their emotions, moods, body language, tone of voice and general responses to be able to communicate with them in a way that enables emotional connection.

Pearce (2009) describes attunement as:

the process by which an attachment figures tune in to the expressed emotion of the infant and reflect the same or a very similar emotion back to the infant. This connection to the infant's emotional experience is communicated by attachment figures through tone of voice, facial expression and gesture. (p.30)

When parents are able to attune to their babies' needs, by matching their emotional responses and giving words to those in a tone that is warm and nurturing, those babies are able to grow up feeling more understood and secure. When parents attune to their kids, and notice the unspoken 'vibe' of their children, they are more likely to open up and be more honest about how they feel and what's going on. Often dinner time can be a good time to scan the unspoken vibe of the school age children and see their faces, body language and general atmosphere to see how they may be doing. Sometimes eating can change their mood and at other times there are things going on for the child that they need us as adults to make space to help them explore.

As a trainer, I need to be attuned because if I don't notice the small signs that the people listening need a break, I lose their interest. It's more important to me to watch their responses and check they are tracking with me, than to just stick to my teaching plan, so that I can then adapt to their needs such as the temperature of the room, the need for coffee or talking, etc.

Another theory that sits alongside attachment theory and the skill of attunement is called mentalization, which was developed by Peter Fonagy and colleagues (2002). This is a concept that refers to the ability to reflect and understand our own state of mind and to understand what we are feeling and why. When the caregivers model this behaviour to the children and also help them to reflect and understand their feelings, it seems to become a strong foundation for emotional regulation. When a child hasn't had that repetitive experience from an adult in their early years, it can be difficult for them to reflect and understand their experience which can lead them to struggle not only with their feelings but also with understanding others' experiences.

Emotional connection

To help strengthen an attachment with a child, the primary ingredients are emotional connection and responsiveness and there are several things that we can do as adults, depending on the child's age. Essentially the emotional connection needs time to develop, but this time can be in lots of small bursts rather than long periods of time. Babies who know that their primary caregiver will respond quickly and consistently to distress in a nurturing way feel able to explore their feelings longer term with the same adult. When their needs are not quickly met in a nurturing way, coping mechanisms are developed which then hinder other relational intimacy and emotional expression. As they get older we still need to be responsive and attentive to them and have the ability for them to feel emotionally connected to us.

Johnny and his mum's story

Johnny was eight years old and loved to play and loved trains but he also struggled with his friendships and preferred to play on his own. When people interrupted his play he would get annoyed and angry and so few children wanted to play with him. When his mum wanted him at the table for dinner she would shout and expect him to come and he often wouldn't. She was so good at making sure that all his practical needs were met that it hadn't occurred to her that Johnny hadn't had many relational exchanges with her where he had learned to negotiate and feel listened to. Through a coffee with a friend, mum realised her own mother had been great at meeting her physical needs but not her emotional needs and now she was repeating this with Johnny. Now she tried to walk over to him rather than shout and then get down with him and his trains for a little while before asking him to come for dinner. Johnny then walked in with her happily to eat. She realised that the tiny exchanges she made by smiling and getting down to his height helped him feel connected and listened to and valued. Soon he was interacting better with the other kids and he chatted more to mum each day.

The key pointers to building emotional connection and you as a place of security and safety are:

- Don't ignore their demands for attention – always look at them and explain if you need a moment before you can respond. Be their safe place and security.

- Always assume the best about them. When they are irritating – breathe deeply and relax – it will be over soon!

- Offer emotional connection with your facial expression, eye contact, body posture and tone of voice. Get to know what they need from you to help them feel safe and calm.

- Don't be too intense, anxious or fearful about getting this wrong! It should be fun. When things are intense and awful, picture yourself telling another parent and laughing together. Just don't laugh yet… And remember that none of us get this parenting stuff perfect. We are trying our best!

- Be playful! Find the best way of playing with your child according to their age and interests and find something you can enjoy together.

- Be age appropriate! Use the tone of voice and play style that's appropriate for the age of your child. Don't keep them 'young and cute' when they are ready to grow up and don't make them feel grown up when they are young and should be free from responsibility!

- Affirm and praise them for specific things so they know you noticed and care.

The following is an excerpt from my *Simple Guide to Understanding Shame in Children* (2018) where I explore how shame can be hugely detrimental in relationships but can be worked through in the context of a relationship where there is healthy emotional connection.

- With children, to spend time with someone to help them feel emotionally connected and less alone and isolated and misunderstood, find somewhere where they feel emotionally safe – their home or somewhere where they don't feel embarrassed or watched by peers.

- Make sure you think through your body posture. With young children, be on their eye level. Younger children prefer it if you kneel down or sit down and play with toys whereas some older children and adolescents may feel uncomfortable looking at you as it may feel too intense so focus on a shared task. That could be anything from building a LEGO® model, cooking, making something, colouring, mending a bike, gardening, shopping, etc.

- Concentrate on being relaxed and calm because if you are anxious, they will sense it and want to please you or be scared and nervous. Then enjoy the time with them so that you can naturally show empathy for their worries or hurts, show kindness and tell them how much you believe the best about them. Be encouraging about specific things they have achieved or have chosen not to have done. General encouraging sentences such as 'you are so great' can be nice but isn't as effective as specific encouragement such as 'you did so well to persist then instead of giving up. I'm really proud of you' or 'You know I noticed you walk away when that kid tried to tease/ hurt/poke/laugh at you. That was amazing. Well done.'

- Make sure that they feel your genuine concern, empathy, patience and care with your words and the time you take to be with them and by making sure that your facial responses match your words! A grumpy face saying 'I care' is just confusing for them and an adult looking at the clock all the time makes the child feel like they are not important!

- When an adult helps a child feel emotionally connected and cared for their feelings of shame become less powerful and begin to decrease. (de Thierry 2018, pp.90–1)

Reflection points

- What is it like to be listened to and when others are attuned to you?

- What makes it hard to attune to the children you care for?

- What things are your best ingredients for spending time with a child and emotionally connecting to them?

Chapter Three

THE BRAIN SCIENCE AROUND ATTACHMENT

Healthy attachment experiences enable babies to build confidence, and encourage them to explore their world. This is the primary way that they learn how to deal with stress and fear and will impact their approach to such experiences into adulthood. Levine and Kline (2006) explain the foundational experience of the primary caregiver 'tuning in' to the needs of the baby:

> What is even more astounding is how this emotional growth between a mother and her newborn is the catalyst that 'turns on' the infant brain, releasing chemicals, proteins, enzymes, and other elements that actually shape both the structure and capacity of the brain. (p.308)

Understanding the threat response

It can be helpful to understand the natural physiological response to threat and fear that begins before we are born, so that we can understand how we respond to fear. A simple overview of our brain's structure can help us to understand the behaviour that is influenced by fear, threat and terror. To make it simple we could see our brains as being in three main parts. The brainstem is an area in our brain at the back of our head where our necks and head joins and is the oldest part of the brain. When we feel fear, it makes us respond with fight (aggression, self defensive behaviour), flight (running away, hiding) or freeze (not moving or becoming internalised). When the brainstem (or primitive brain) responds with any of these immediate and instinctive reactions, it triggers a whole load of other reactions. Immediately a part of our brain called the amygdala, which is located in the limbic brain or middle brain, alerts the body to the fear and then the body starts pumping adrenaline and cortisol to give us enough strength either to fight the threat or run from the threat or freeze like a rabbit in headlights and not move despite the threat.

Whilst this physiological response and extra energy would be useful if there was a giant bear or lion, it can be a challenge to babies when they are scared because they are hungry and need milk, or if they are scared because their parent hasn't responded to their cries, because their brain responds to the fear with these reactions regardless of what the fear is! It can make babies cry louder, and make toddlers hit and kick or have tantrums or worse still it can eventually make a child become unresponsive to the adults caring for them. When children feel fear because of hearing a door bang whilst at school or when someone drops a plate in the school canteen and they cry and run, it can be because their subconscious can't differentiate from the fear they felt when they heard an argument at home or when their cries weren't answered with the comforting arms of a safe parent. This threat response can release the energy and stress hormones, which cause them to be unable to sit still and they start running, wriggling, shouting, giggling, or being aggressive or silly.

How the threat response affects behaviour

The child wouldn't know that they are responding to fear, or the sound of the door banging or the plate being dropped. They will probably not know how they feel at all because when this instinctive reaction happens in our brain we all actually immediately stop thinking rationally! This is because when the brainstem and amygdala react to fear, and adrenaline and cortisol are released, we struggle to use the part of our brain called the prefrontal cortex that is responsible for thinking, being rational, reasonable, thinking and speaking. That's why when we ask children why they reacted in some negative ways they look blankly or shrug their shoulders. It's also why we can say things or do things that seem inappropriate when we feel fear. Our prefrontal cortex (the thinking, rational, reflective brain) goes 'offline' when we feel frightened and we act instinctively. Toddlers may hit and scream when they are hungry; we may hide when the doorbell goes even when we know a friend is due for coffee or a child may freeze when a teacher asks to see them even when they know they haven't done anything wrong. Our threat response takes over our body to try and protect us from the danger it has noticed.

When a baby or child experiences the threat response and is comforted and calmed by an adult who has a warm and kind tone of voice, gentle touch, helpful words and a sense of emotional connection rather than rejection or anger, then they can learn to self-regulate. If they are not comforted when they feel frightened or threatened then their behaviour can escalate and become more challenging because they are feeling increased fear the more times that they are not being helped to be calm and feel safe. Attachment relationships are key in providing these early and continuing experiences of safety and calm in the midst of fear and threat.

> Negative emotional states can be shared as the adult then helps the child to reduce these states and soothe his distress. Helping a child learn that he will not be emotionally abandoned during these moments and that he can learn to understand and soothe his painful emotional state is an important role for the attachment figure to play. (Siegel 2001, p.2)

The attachment chemicals that are released in birth and the stress chemicals that can hinder them

A baby in the womb is designed to experience oxytocin whilst growing as the mum strokes and chats to her unborn child as she waits for the birth. Oxytocin is a neurotransmitter and a hormone that is produced in the hypothalamus; it is then transported to and secreted from the pituitary gland at the base of the brain.

It is often called the 'love chemical' or 'attachment hormone' because it is released during hugging, childbirth or when two people are experiencing emotional connection. If oxytocin wasn't naturally produced in childbirth there would be significantly less births due to the level of pain, but the hormone causes 'happy highs' that enable the mum to 'fall in love' with their child rather than resent them for the pain endured. If the mum experiences significant stress during the pregnancy then the baby may be experiencing higher levels of cortisol rather than oxytocin and this can harm the baby's brain. If then at birth the mum is highly stressed and the baby is hugely stressed because it is arriving into a cold, brightly lit world that feels new and strange, attachment problems can occur unless we recognise the potential longer term impact of stress going unresolved. Hopefully, to avoid any attachment problems, the mum immediately greets her baby with relief because both the mum and baby are flooded with oxytocin leading to the baby feeling safe and the mum feeling elated. It is in her arms that a baby should begin the journey of learning that stress and fear is tolerable because the mum will then comfort and bring safety. This leads to the mum usually being the primary attachment figure and therefore the source of safety and comfort.

When there is a traumatic birth or the baby is separated from the mother and the natural chemicals process is hindered, the baby can still recover and attachment can still take place. Intentional work to enable the attachment relationship to form is important and there are ways of helping the newborn, for example using clothes that smell of mum to snuggle near them. If it is at all possible, the baby will respond well with the familiar sound of mum's voice, or the voice of the dad or another person who was a familiar voice during the pregnancy. The attachment continues to develop as oxytocin is released when the parent and baby look into each other's eyes, laugh and chat.

Sarah's story

My Sarah wouldn't go to school as she hated leaving me. Every morning she was 'peeled off me' by the teacher, leaving both of us in floods of tears. I realised that if I popped on a scarf every day and wore it the whole way to school, Sarah could take that with her and it smelled of me and it would be a comfort to her before she got busy with her school activities. I also gave her a heart shaped button that I sewed into her pocket so that she could feel the shape and texture of it and remember how much I loved her whenever she felt sad or was missing me.

Social relationships

Oxytocin continues to be an important hormone that is released when the baby, and then toddler and child, are comforted or laugh together or share pleasure.

The orbitofrontal cortex area of the brain is busy dealing with emotional responses and behaviours that are located in the subconscious and it is the centre of social relationships. The prefrontal cortex is like the control centre for the other regions of the brain that hold emotional reactions and impulses and it is the part of the brain that only develops after birth and only in the context of relationships. Researchers would describe it as 'experience dependent'. The continuous and repetitive co-regulation between a parent or carer and the baby or toddler helps them lay down patterns, which naturally develop into self-regulation of their emotions and reactions. These experiences are full of oxytocin release and develop the orbitofrontal cortex. Cozolino speaks of the experience of healthy attachment relationships where it is:

> the day to day experience of young children as they go through cycles of regulation, dysregulation and regulation, their parents serving as external frontal lobes, helping them to navigate their emotional ups and downs of life. Repeating this experience thousands of times creates an unconscious experience of regulation. (2006, p.260)

The concept of rupture and repair

The good news is that a child needs to experience and learn about the reality of what is called 'rupture and repair' of the attachment relationship. When a child has to be told 'no' and the parent looks cross, the child in that instance can feel abandoned and terrified unless they have slowly learned through experience that they can expect a repair to that momentary rupture in emotional connection. The repair, if speedy and genuine, is usually full of an oxytocin release and can actually build a healthy attachment. When a child has very zealous or anxious parents and they jump to every cry and need, actually the child doesn't experience the joy of the repair after the rupture and can become unfamiliar with ruptures and become anxious! Therefore as long as the ruptures are natural, not neglectful or nasty or repetitive and as long as the adult repairs with genuine warmth and empathy and apology if necessary, then the baby and child can learn to relax when things go slightly wrong in the hope that, minutes later, the attachment will be 'fixed'. The baby and child should learn to develop a general trust that their needs will be met and if misattunement occurs, there will be a repair.

> Just as the child produces cortisol in response to the parent's face, so too does the dispersion of cortisol depend on a changed expression on the parent's face. The young child can't do this for himself, so if parents don't restore attunement and regulation, he may remain stuck in a state of arousal. (Gerhardt 2004, p.49)

This rupture and repair should be a strengthening experience in the attachment relationship.

Reflection points

- What behaviours would you expect from a child who is feeling threatened?

- What chemicals are released that strengthen the attachment relationship and how can you produce more?

Chapter Four

THE SAFE PLACE AND CO-REGULATION

There seems to be sudden attention on the concept of self-regulation in schools at the moment. Adults are realising that when a child cannot 'control' or regulate their emotions, reactions and responses, it leads to a classroom or playground being a place of anarchy! However, what seems to be lost in some places amidst the urgency is the knowledge that self-regulation actually develops out of co-regulation. Ideally, children experienced the continual, repetitive emotional regulation repetitively with an attachment figure whilst growing up in their first five years. If they did, then they have got a well-worn path of knowing how to soothe, calm and regulate their emotions, responses and reactions. The voice of the adult(s) who helped them calm and be comforted by co-regulating with them becomes like an internal voice that enables them to do exactly what they would have done with their attachment figure if they were there with them. Cozolino speaks of the long term impact of the early attachment relationship:

> Optimal sculpting of the prefrontal cortex through healthy early relationships allows us to think well of ourselves, trust others, regulate our emotions, maintain positive experiences and utilize our emotional and intellectual intelligence in moment to moment problem solving. (2006, p.14)

If the child didn't have that early positive co-regulation experience then they are often offered it in school settings. This is because without the ability to self-regulate, the child's impulsive behaviour can be problematic in a classroom. The co-regulation offered is usually done through identifying an academic need, such as additional literacy or maths lessons that can facilitate a small, co-regulatory experience for the child. In these quiet, calm moments where the adult uses soothing tones to speak about the subject and is encouraging and uses affirmations and motivations, the child relaxes and feels soothed and safe. The same adult could then use the same tone of voice, affirmation, motivation and general approach when the child then had a 'melt down' of some kind because they had built up some attachment relationship over repetition during their one-to-one work. As adults we are able to co-regulate with any child in our care who needs that developmental experience, either because they missed out on it between birth and five years old due to stress, trauma or unavailability of the parent or because the child has experienced some difficult challenges that have unsettled them and led them to need further co-regulation to strengthen their ability to self-regulate. Research is beginning to link evidence of the vital role of the primary caregiver in helping the children learn how to regulate their emotions and behaviour.

> Caregiver behaviors are thought to contribute significantly to the development of self-regulation. Children rely on caregivers to regulate their state, arousal, and behavior during infancy and gradually develop self-sufficiency in managing their own actions and emotions into early childhood; it is the regulation provided by caregivers that presents children with increasingly complex social, emotional, and cognitive experiences that allow them to practice self-regulating. (Sameroff 2010)

What is co-regulation and how do I do it?

Co-regulation requires the adult to be emotionally available, present and kind, warm and empathetic whilst a child is having an emotional reaction. In these pressured moments, the adult is able to attune to the child's dysregulated state, bring a sense of calm and strength into the chaos and eventually, with patience and confidence, facilitate a de-escalation of emotion and behaviour. For an adult to be able to de-escalate things when a child is having such a melt down, it helps if the adult and child have regularly spent time together with the adult being intentional about emotionally connecting through play, laughter and talking.

The best way to develop a positive attachment relationship that can co-regulate with the child is to spend some quality time with them, in a one-to-one setting, focusing on some activity that you can enjoy together, where as the adult, you are choosing to be undistracted and instead fully attune to the child and their needs, emotions, reactions and responses. It doesn't have to be long periods of time, but enough for you both to experience that emotional connection that causes laughter, smiles and playful fun. This builds up the 'muscles' of self-regulation as the adult gently responds to the different emotions and gives words to the experience and sense. Then when a child is upset, frustrated, angry or having an emotional outburst, they are familiar with an adult focusing on their response in an empathetic, kind, nurturing way where they can question what the child is needing, in order to help them explore their emotions and reactions. The process of co-regulation is one where the child feels known by their attachment figure and safe from overwhelming emotions and experiences.

The signals sent by each member of an attuned dyad [a pair of individuals] are directly responsive in quality and timing with each other. These attuned communications often have their foundation in the nonverbal signals that are shared between two individuals. Eye contact, facial expression, tone of voice, bodily gestures and timing and intensity of response are all fundamental aspects of nonverbal signals. These primary emotions can be seen as the 'music of the mind'. Each person may come to 'feel felt' by the other. (Siegel 2001, p.2)

When it's been difficult to co-regulate

Parents who are not comfortable at co-regulating with their children can end up leaving the child in a distressed state for too long to avoid being affected by the negative emotion. If as the adults in the midst of a child's emotional outburst, they themselves find the feeling of powerlessness too scary and the negative feelings they are both experiencing too difficult, they may walk away or become angry. Sadly, the child is then left feeling abandoned and frightened, which can escalate their responses. It can also be the same when children are happy and excited. The parents may be uncomfortable with such exuberance and rather than share with their delight can shame, blame, mock or tell off the children, causing the same deep sense of confusion, abandonment and sadness.

It has been noted that when children are not able to regularly and repetitively practise co-regulation with an adult in the context of an attachment relationship they grow up into adults who:

seem to lack the more complex regulatory strategies that are associated with prefrontal development. Instead of actively solving problems with other people, talking things through, confident that some resolution can be found, they tend either to withdraw from people or attack them aggressively. (Gerhardt 2004, p.130)

Exploring the concept of the safe place

Bowlby described the primary attachment figure as the 'safe place from which to explore the world'. That person should be the primary place that the child feels safe and secure. We see in a toddler that they often run off to explore something but turn around to check their attachment figure is present and watching. Sometimes they run back for a cuddle before running off again. This repetitive pattern of reuniting and checking that the adult is there enables the child to have the confidence to explore and still feel safe. As the child gets older it becomes more about the adult picking them up after school ready to listen to them and meet some of their need to process their experiences and have their physical needs met, and maybe staying near them as they fall asleep at night. These experiences all build up the sense of internal safety for a child that helps them grow in confidence until they don't need the adult any more. It is not enough for a child to be safe – they need to feel safe – and it's not enough for a child to be secure – they need to feel secure.

Paul's story

Paul hadn't really ever felt safe at home because there was lots of chaos and difficulty and so he struggled to feel safe in school too. He used to arrive and run around the whole school and then be agitated and distracting when the other children were happily learning. The teacher arranged for him to see a TA called Mrs Scarlett for an hour a day to do some work that enabled him to have co-regulation. She could help him name emotions, learn some calming tools like breathing games and they could also laugh together and enjoy books. Soon this became his safe place and she became an attachment figure who offered a sense of emotional security to him. He loved his hour sessions but also knew if he was upset about something he could go and find Mrs Scarlett, who would always help him feel safe again. When he got to Year 6 the school had to think very carefully about the transition to secondary school and needed to introduce a mentor from there who could slowly gain his trust in his weekly visit, in order to lessen the stress of losing the daily contact. He still pops into his old school for tea with Mrs Scarlett now though and they go through a photo book she made of things they made and got up to in the special room.

_____

School as the safe place

Whilst it is ideal that children and young people have an attachment figure or two, for some, school becomes the safe place and where they experience attachment relationships. It can be a warm, caring place where the child can feel known and cared for by familiar adults who offer consistent, repetitive co-regulating relationships that enable the child to feel calm and safe. Sometimes home can be too volatile, difficult and unsafe and so the child needs to learn co-regulation in the context of other relationships. This can happen intentionally or sometimes it happens naturally. When a child has an attachment to a school several things need to be thought through. There needs to be attention on the child having 'access' to the familiar key adult that has co-regulated with them for a period of time because changes here can cause attachment rupture that can lead to terror and therefore an escalation of challenging behaviour. Whilst adults need to be careful with boundaries to avoid exhaustion and a dependency on them by a child, at the same time we need to recognise that if an attachment relationship has been built, then it needs to be added to and not replaced. If the child feels abandoned by the attachment figure or, worse still, another child has access to them and they don't, you can expect chaos and anger to be expressed! School or youth groups, and other places where children and young people can be known by adults who care, can be life-transforming places where attachment relationships can be facilitated naturally.

> Teachers can facilitate a positive relational experience which can change the expectations of children who have not had the benefit of enjoying an adult's care and nurture. This doesn't need to take additional time but just the recognition that every smile, every look of affirmation, every validation of a feeling and every time comfort is offered, can change the neurological pathways of a child's brain forever and therefore change their future. (de Thierry 2015, p.125)

The child who doesn't have a safe place at home needs to be at school and be known, see photos of themselves on the wall with other kids, know that the adults will support and help them when life can be overwhelming and will listen and care for them. When it comes to a transition into senior school, the child needs to know that they can pop back any time and experience again their emotional safety and security. A good transition can take half a year, because the child needs help to collect memories and think through the transition. The attachment figure ideally needs to have regular visits with the child to the new school and preferably transfer the attachment to a new adult who can care for them and know them.

Reflection points

- What has the co-regulation experience been for the child you are caring for?

- Where would they describe as their safe place and why?

- What could you do to help your child gain skills in self-regulation?

Chapter Five

WHAT IS AN UNHEALTHY ATTACHMENT BEHAVIOUR?

When a child has not had the experience of consistent co-regulation and emotional attunement from a primary caregiver, they can develop attachment difficulties. There needs to be a recognition here of the level of grief for many parents about their lack of knowledge about this subject, or their lack of capacity due to their own trauma or challenging circumstances, to ensure that we are not shaming or blaming parents. A lot of parents would love to have been able to provide such healthy early experiences but had to survive terror, difficult relationships, poverty, juggling other crippling demands, their own mental health challenges or early trauma or sudden experiences that meant they were not able to be all that they wanted to be. Life can be difficult and blaming ourselves or shaming others doesn't help any of us recover or strengthen, so as we continue please remember that the parents probably tried their best with what they had at the time.

Attachment behaviours

Ainsworth (Ainsworth *et al.* 1978) used the procedure called the Strange Situation to research attachment behaviours and she came up with four that she asserted people formed internally:

- secure

- insecure-avoidant

- insecure-ambivalent

- disorganised/disorientated.

We have already explored how a secure attachment behaviour is formed. Essentially, the other less positive behaviours are formed due to experiences in the baby's early life that caused either confusion or distress.

Children who exhibit the **insecure-avoidant attachment behaviour** usually appear independent and can seem unbothered by their attachment figure. When they are upset they don't tend to seek out their attachment figure for comfort. Maybe their internal belief about attachment is 'I don't need anyone anyway'. They usually hide their emotions and so often the level of anxiety and hopelessness they may be feeling is not noticed by adults around them until they become older and they begin to explode or suddenly become emotionally reactive in times of stress or fear.

Children who exhibit **insecure-ambivalent attachment behaviours** (or preoccupied attachment behaviour) usually display clingy behaviour and seem to be difficult to soothe and settle. They can appear to be needy, frustrated, angry and clingy. Maybe their internal belief about attachment is, 'I'm really upset so don't leave me but now I'm still frightened so help me'. They often seem to exaggerate their emotions and behaviour to try and get their needs met. They usually need to be noticed by adults who could care for them and desperately want their emotional connection and so they can hide their feelings of worthlessness and terror and appear angry and disruptive instead.

No parent wants to facilitate an unhealthy attachment behaviour in their children and usually they have tried their best, but often they didn't have the tools themselves to offer a secure, repetitive relationship due to their own lack of positive early years experience with an adult. When an adult hasn't experienced co-regulation with a primary attachment figure then they can find it hard to co-regulate with their own children. This can lead to negative attachment behaviours in the child.

> Insecure attachments tend to come about because parents find it hard to respond adequately to their babies, for a variety of reasons. Mostly this is because their own difficulties in regulating their own feelings get passed on to their children. The parents themselves have not had their baby needs met and so are unable to provide this for their own babies. (Gerhardt 2004, p.88)

How this impacts on the child's behaviour

When a child is struggling with their understanding of adults and trying to make sense of their world, they communicate their uncertainty or fear through behaviour and not words. A child struggling with attachment difficulties will often be challenging in their relationships with adults due to either anxiety and fear or confusion and frustration or anger and sadness.

Behaviour that could actually be fear-based could be as diverse as a child appearing to be withdrawn and shy or aggressive and controlling or sarcastic and loud or nasty to others. Behaviour that could be due to sadness may be similar. Sadness often looks like anger and fear can look like sadness. Anger is often actually fear, terror or sadness.

Experiencing negative attachment relationships can cause a child to form an 'internal working model' or 'schema' that causes them to relate to everyone else from that negative foundation. The child then expects all adults to be confusing, angry, untrustworthy, un-attuned or uninterested in them, as their original attachment figure was, and so they are left trying to navigate their world without having had the experiences that were able to lead to a subconscious sense of security and safety. The insecure attachments that were formed in the context of the child's early experience are often then reaffirmed when their sadness causes the behaviour that leads to them being criticised and rejected by other adults.

The child is desperate to find an adult relationship where they can feel safety and security and from there be able to explore who they are and make sense of the world, but they don't have the tools to know how to develop such a thing and often don't know it's even a possibility. There is a saying that 'those who need love the most ask for it in the most unloving of ways'.

Disorganised attachment behaviour

This term and how to identify it in children has caused a lot of discussion since the days of Ainsworth, and particularly in the last few years. The term 'fright without solution' was coined initially to suggest the notion that some toddlers and younger children were observed showing, at first sight, odd, confusing, conflicting or even fearful behaviours towards a parent or carer in situations where one would have expected them to have sought comfort, protection or reassurance from that adult, for example when hearing a loud bang or a dog bark. Often children would then be discussed as potentially having 'disorganised attachment' due to these behaviours. However, researchers now believe that these behaviours are more complex and can result from the child being frightened of but also for their carer (for example, if they are depressed or experiencing bereavement).

These researchers also believe that the behaviours that are thought of as showing 'disorganised attachment' could also develop in other ways such as a specific condition in the child or even a genetic factor.

As with all attachment behaviours that we have explored in this book, the good news is that children, young people and adults can change as the neural pathways can change the subconscious expectation and understanding of relationships, which then leads to changes in behaviour.

It is important to remember that this book is aimed at helping adults reflect and learn so that they can seek professional help if the behaviours are concerning, and can understand the challenges and so work together to help the child. The best scenario for a child is that they have nurturing adults offering positive attachment relationships working alongside professionals who can offer formal assessments and clinical assessments that can evidence change and recovery. For a summary see Shemmings (2016b) and for some additional insights and observations from John Bowlby's, until recently, unpublished reflections see Reisz, Duschinsky and Siegel (2017).

What children need from these attachment relationships are long-term, patient, kind, nurturing, emotionally attuned and consistent adults who don't retaliate when they are rejected, hated and hurt by these children, who may reject adults before they have to face the possibility of being rejected again.

Crittenden (2005), on the other hand, argues that there is no such thing as 'disorganised attachment' because she says that children behave in ways to protect themselves in the face of danger. She says that attachment is not the problem – the problem is the *danger*. Therefore she asserts that children who can appear disorganised and volatile in their attachment relationship are usually shifting from one attachment behaviour to another according to what helps them get their needs met the most. Therefore the attachment behaviour is highly adaptive.

Zack and his mum's story

When my adopted son Zack was just over 18 months old, I noticed that unlike other friends' babies he didn't cling to me, come back to me at a playgroup, look me in the eye or in any way enjoy being held. He didn't seem to like me playing with him, reading with him or trying to chat with him. He seemed to be always on the go and never relaxing or peaceful. He was being increasingly difficult and I was feeling exhausted.

I realised it could be an attachment difficulty and knew that babies can have trouble attaching to their adoptive parents because they have been traumatised or neglected, and that they view the adopted parent as another adult who may or may not abandon them. Though they are young, deep down they believe very strongly that the only ones they can trust are themselves.

I became more conscious to take every opportunity to love Zack and show him that I loved him by being persistent. It was hard and at first, it didn't seem to work and he became increasingly less able to be with anyone as he was disruptive and not relationally 'normal'. We had to be so committed to being consistent and finding ways to help him know that we were not going to leave him ever. When his language skills increased, that became easier. Zack became more able to express his emotions verbally and understand himself and then became less disruptive and volatile. He began to show warmth towards us and as he engaged with therapy he was able to express some deep fears and process them together with me and the therapist. He's 11 now and such a great kid. He still has his wobbles but is emotionally intelligent and can verbalise his needs which makes me so proud.

———————

How possible is it for children to develop a healthy attachment behaviour having had attachment difficulties?

A child's brain is most flexible and adaptable to new learning in the first five years and therefore, their developing brain has the possibility of changing dramatically. As new experiences are repeated, new neural pathways are formed which change behaviour and emotions and subconscious responses and reactions. When a child has experienced anxious or ambivalent attachment with their primary caregiver, they can learn new attachment behaviours as they experience positive, repetitive, affirming, nurturing relationships with adults. The co-regulation and emotional attunement that we explored earlier is the pathway to a child developing a healthy brain, subconscious and future. In further chapters we'll explore how to build positive experiences when a child has experienced attachment trauma.

Reflection points

- What is your attachment behaviour?

- Have you experienced a child asking you for love in the most unloving ways?

- What can you do to help children feel safe with you?

Chapter Six

PARENTING THAT CAN HINDER A HEALTHY ATTACHMENT

Life can be challenging for adults with the juggling of work, relationships and responsibilities. Add parenting onto that list and some can find it extremely challenging to remain calm and consistent. Poverty, unemployment or challenging work can bring stress that causes parenting to become a real challenge. When life is easy and calm, parenting is an easier role to fully enter into with energy, whereas it can become exhausting when other areas of life are full of stress. Time becomes limited for the parent to process and make sense of all that they feel, think and experience and yet often many of the usual things they may have done to recover may not be available any more. This can lead to a parent being anxious or depressed or struggling to juggle the demands. Of course, as adults, our own attachment pattern can have a massive influence on our experience of building attachment relationships with children. We need to take time to reflect on our own attachment experiences so that we can be intentional in building healthy attachments rather than falling into default, subconscious patterns of behaviour.

Anxious parenting

When the adult is anxious, the children can often 'pick up' the atmosphere and way of approaching life. Anxiety can limit risk and freedom and when a child senses a parent's anxiety it can hinder their ability to be carefree and innocent. A child learns to be anxious in an atmosphere of anxiety and therefore they can find it harder to experience their primary attachment figure as safe, secure and trustworthy to protect them. When a parent can take some time to regulate their own emotions, process their own feelings and experiences then they are better able to offer their child an anxiety free childhood experience.

> ...have you noticed that when you're nervous or stressed out, your kids will often be that way too? Scientists call this 'emotional contagion'. The internal states of others – from joy and playfulness to sadness and fear – directly affect our own state of mind. We soak other people into our own inner world. (Siegel 2011, p.125)

Helicopter and controlling parenting

Helicopter parenting is a form of anxious parenting where the child does not have the liberty to leave their parent or carer to explore the world but instead is either told to or is made to feel that they have to remain near to the adult. Usually this is because the adult is scared that something bad will happen and would rather always be in control to try and protect the child and prevent anything frightening happening. Sadly, although this could sound kind and caring, it actually stops the child from being able to learn lessons about life and independence that are developmentally appropriate. It is often a very subtle message to the children from the parents that they must stay close to their parent and not explore due to the danger that they may experience and, whilst it is important for a child to grow in an understanding of boundaries, they can also learn anxiety about the world from an early age that can be damaging. A research study (Perry *et al.* 2018) that focused on 'over controlling parenting' during toddlerhood found that a greater desire for independence due to lack of ability to exert choices often puts toddlers in situations of increasing emotional challenge and complexity that can lead them to lack in self-regulation as they grow older:

> If parents try to exert too much control over these situations and step in before children try to handle the challenge independently, or physically keep children from these frustrating or fearful contexts altogether, they may, unintentionally, hinder the development of children's independent self-regulatory abilities. For example, if an over controlling parent removes a young child from a situation where, for a successful peer interaction, she needs to control her emotions/behaviour and share a toy, she may not develop the skills to navigate that situation in socially appropriate ways when a parent is not present. (Perry *et al.* 2018)

Some parents or carers are somewhat over-anxious about their children achieving things that they weren't able to achieve as children and we refer to this as 'living through them'. Children can feel huge pressure to live up to the expectations of their primary attachment figure and can feel anxious about 'failing them' or disappointing them. Again this is often a 'secret' anxiety because children find that difficult to put into words. We need to emphasise that we are aiming at supporting the children in becoming the best individual, unique person that they are and not a copy of anyone else.

Lack of emotional intelligence

As attachment figures for children we can help them best when we are able to be emotionally regulated and intelligent. When we are able to explore our inner thoughts, reactions, responses and defence mechanisms then we are more able to guide the children we are caring for through to emotional intelligence. We have already explored that the adult offering consistent availability and emotional connection is the vital ingredient in all attachment relationships. The consequence for a child who doesn't experience this is that they can be left with a lack of emotional literacy, emotional intelligence and also a strong feeling of sadness, loneliness, abandonment and confusion. If as carers or parents it's too difficult to offer such important experiences for the child, then other adults can be brought into the child's life to fulfil that need and the hindrance can be explored in a simple way so that the child doesn't feel rejected.

Domineering and authoritarian parenting

When the child grows up with a sense of fear about their parent's anger or displeasure with any behaviour that is less than perfect, they will struggle to form a healthy attachment. If the parent creates a culture of them being in charge and the children having no opinion worth listening to, the child feels powerless and devalued. Often the anger is below the surface of households with an authoritarian or dominant parent, but the child notices the facial expressions of displeasure and the clear affirmation of expected behaviour. When fear is the primary experience for a child, whether they realise it or not, they will struggle to form positive attachment relationships with adults due to a strong fear of anger, fear of failure and fear of disapproval.

> When a parent's own emotional needs are too dominating, their child's needs cannot be met and this can also lead to a child having difficulties learning to regulate their own emotions. However, if a child experiences caring, relational interactions that are continually repeated and repeated, then they are able to trust that relational process and consequently have the emotional resilience to explore more relationships and new situations. (de Thierry 2015, p.53)

Lack of boundaries from the parent or carer

If a child grows up with the parent figure relating to them as their best friend, the child can feel confused and frightened. A child needs the adult to take responsibility and hold clear boundaries around behaviour. When the parent doesn't do this, either because they are being relaxed and letting 'anything happen' or maybe because they think 'they'll learn themselves eventually', the child can feel too much responsibility and not enough guidance. A child needs the adult to guide them and help them make sense of the world and this takes time to talk and play and co-regulate their emotions and reactions.

Emotionally absent parenting

A child can feel rejected and abandoned when the parent is not emotionally attentive to them. Even if the basic needs of the child are met, such as food, drink, toys and education, the child needs an emotional connection to become emotionally healthy. If the child is left without a primary caregiver giving attention, time and intentional regular, repetitive and nurturing care and play, then they will learn dysfunctional coping mechanisms to cope with the void of healthy emotional experience. The parent who can help the child to explore his or her own feelings and experiences enables the child to develop positive, strong and healthy emotional literacy in the context of a positive relationship. A child who has emotionally absent primary caregivers often doesn't know what they are lacking but instead seeks to fill the void through other things that bring a sense of relief or they shut down their feelings and become emotionally numb.

A busy family story

We have three kids and we really love them all and so wanted to be good parents. Because we so wanted to do the best that we could, my partner worked long hours whilst I did some extra work in the evenings from home to make a bit of extra money so that we could get the kids some of what they wanted. There was always something! I think we were quite normal as a family and things seemed to be great until the older two kids began to show signs of being angry and not listening to us or doing anything we asked. This behaviour seemed to get worse and we were so shocked and embarrassed as they started to behave in ways that other parents were commenting on – volatile, running off, screaming, saying they hated us, etc. When we got some help, the parenting support worker helped us to think through the kids' experience with us. We realised that actually our middle child might well be feeling left out as he had no time with either of us really, and the eldest had actually felt pressure that we hadn't noticed because we'd both been really stressed and actually we often got ill with it all and had to have days off in bed. We just hadn't seen how much she was carrying responsibility for the whole family even though she was only eight years old because we were so focused on working to get them what they needed. As we learned more about the role of the primary attachment figure and the needs of the child to have emotional connection, we began to prioritise having one-to-one time with each of them. We played games and listened to them as they began to chat. With the eldest we took her out for milkshakes and told her we were sorry that she felt pressure that she shouldn't have had to feel and helped her to feel valued. Now they are all completely different and happy again and they tell us when they need time with us – although we still have our weekly play dates. Spending intentional time with us one on one seemed to have a hugely powerful effect of peace in our house!

When the child becomes the carer

When a child grows up with a parent who is struggling, they can often take on the role of caring for the adult. This can often not be recognised as people assess the practical tasks of the family and the adult may well be doing those with consistency. It is damaging when the child feels like they are holding the weight for the emotional well-being of the family and, although it may look loving and kind, being put in this position actually causes the child to feel confused internally as they swap roles with their parent and become the one who carries the responsibility for their adult. It can be damaging to the child, can rob them of a carefree and innocent childhood, and often these children go on to take responsibility for everyone around them for the rest of their lives due to their inbuilt way of relating to others.

When there is abuse in the home

It should go without saying that when a child experiences abuse from the hands of the adult who is meant to be the one looking after them, the damage is significant. This usually causes some kind of attachment difficulties because the child needs their parent and wants to be loyal to their parent, but yet is terrified of them because they are hurting them or not protecting them. We will be exploring this in the following two chapters.

Reflection points

- What negative attachment behaviours do you have to be careful about?

- What do you think the child you are thinking about needs from you the most?

- How do you carve out time to spend reflecting on your inner world and emotional health?

Chapter Seven

ATTACHMENT TRAUMA

With the increase in children being diagnosed
with attachment disorders and the increased use
of the word attachment there has been a common
misunderstanding that to learn about attachment is
to learn about trauma. It is important to understand
the relationship between attachment and trauma
in order to fully grasp the healthy development of
children. Attachment theory gives us the ability to
reflect on the child's internal ability to relate to
adults as safe and trustworthy and understand that
some children struggle with that because of a lack
of early experience, while others find that they have
not experienced positive attachment relationships
but can soon adapt and enjoy them and others have
been traumatised by their attachment figure. When a
child has been traumatised by their attachment figure,
the level of trauma is usually quite severe and the
child's behaviour usually makes that quite clear. This
is when the child has attachment difficulties, which
are trauma based. It is also important to remember
that sometimes children are traumatised and yet they
have positive, healthy attachment relationships and so
offering an 'attachment' based intervention will not

necessarily reduce the symptoms of trauma and in fact can cause some confusion.

The impact of neglect and abuse on attachment

Sadly children can be traumatised by their primary caregiver and attachment figure because they were neglected, emotionally or physically. This causes the child to live with an extraordinary confusion of feeling love and loyalty alongside sadness and abandonment. When the child is abused by the same person who was responsible for caring for them, the consequence for the child is absolute confusion about safety and trust that leads them to form complex defence mechanisms because no one can be trusted. This is the case in situations of parental neglect and abuse.

> It may be paradoxical that the most destructive children are those who try and suppress their feelings. But the most aggressive boys at school are not those who are high in stress hormones but low in them. Their anger simmers beneath the surface, probably outside their awareness. It also probably arose from very early experiences of neglect or chronic hostility, which has affected their stress response. (Gerhardt 2004, p.81)

The impact on relationships

When a child's primary experience of an adult has been either the absence of care and attunement or the terror of being hurt by the one who they naturally turn to for help and rescue it has a long-term impact on their emotions, relationships, learning and well-being. The child cannot choose to make 'good choices' and forgive the parent and understand their behaviour. They are powerless and defenceless and are left experiencing strong and powerful emotions and physiological responses from a primitive threat response that their little bodies cannot tolerate. These strong emotions then cause self-defensive behaviour that attempts to protect their vulnerability and survive in the face of the terror they are experiencing. With their negative behaviour causing further rejection and anger from adults, the strong emotions become more powerful and the behaviour becomes more desperate, whilst still trying to hide the terror and vulnerability that they have to push down until they can't feel it. They desperately need adults to understand these tensions and to patiently know that for them to unfreeze from their state of terror and learn to trust an adult will be a huge challenge, causing them to feel the feeling of powerlessness and vulnerability that they associate with the threat of survival.

> Child maltreatment has a strong impact on attachment. It creates fear without solution for a child because the attachment figure whom the child would approach for protection in times of stress and anxiety, is the same time the source of fright, whether this attachment figure is the perpetrator, a potential perpetrator (in cases of sibling abuse), or failing to protect the child against the perpetrator. (Cyr *et al.* 2010, p.100)

The impact on emotions

When a child depends on adults to keep them safe and protected and guide them through life gently, but actually experiences fear and confusion in the context of the relationship with their primary caregiver, there are strong emotions that result. The child has to cope with strong and powerful feelings of fear, anger, frustration, sadness, and feelings associated with being abandoned, alone and hurt. If they express these and then receive further rejection, scolding and abuse then they bury them deep down inside so that they minimalise the turmoil. Often children tell us about the 'volcano' they feel is inside them and this is usually these strong, buried emotions. When a child carries on their daily life of going to school, trying to have their basic needs met for love, care, food and sleep met, they can be 'explosive' because of the powerful feelings that result from being hurt by adults.

When a child has been emotionally neglected they often feel more confused and lack the understanding of what 'normal care' is like and would probably defend their parents' care. However, when they grow up with an unresponsive parent, they either withdraw and become independent and self sufficient or they become louder and louder until they get the attention of the adult who should be caring for them.

> Children who are described in the attachment literature as 'resistantly' attached tend to dramatise their emotions. They do this in response to parents who are inconsistently emotionally available – whether distracted, absent minded, busy or frequently absent. They capture their parents' attention by amplifying them, but they never quite know if they can get the comfort they need when they need it. (Gerhardt 2004, p.78)

The impact on behaviour

When a child is trying to cope with these strong feelings of fear and confusion, and when they have to be intent on making sure they have their needs met because there is no adult focused on that for them, they can exhibit behaviour that demonstrates their agitation and preoccupation with survival. It makes sense that they may well struggle to concentrate on tasks that are not connected to their survival and demonstrate fear in relationships and expectations from others. Often the child who is in survival mode is in an endless cycle of fear leading to behaviour that causes adults to punish them which leads to further fear leading to further behaviour that causes further punishment. Then they are often labelled bad or difficult children or given a diagnosis that still doesn't help their core needs of having love, care, consistency and nurture provided for them.

> She was driven by fear, unable to think about the consequences of her behaviour. This endless pattern left her ashamed and alone. (Cozolino 2006, p.321)

Joe's mum's story

A friend suggested I go on the Freedom Program and slowly I began to understand that it was not OK for Dave to hit me or shout at me and the kids. I realised we were all terrified of him but my eldest, Joe, he really suffered. He loved his dad but he heard what he called me and saw him hit me and he got hit too. Joe got just like his dad, treating me the same way and he was so angry all the time. I got help to get away, and now Joe gets help to make sense of his confused feelings about me and his dad. It's hard because he reminds me of his dad and makes me feel scared. I'm getting therapy too and I understand that Joe needs me to be calm and consistent with him and he needs me to help him feel safe again.

The impact on learning

A child who struggles to trust adults to care for them will often struggle to focus on learning.

A child who doesn't easily trust adults and is occupied with finding ways to cope with unmet needs can be agitated, unfocused, distracting and aggressive. They can't use the prefrontal cortex to think and learn due to their survival brain taking control. Alternatively the child is withdrawn, quiet, day dreamy and independent because they don't trust other people and are just quietly focused on surviving and having their needs met. When teachers are able to be consistently kind, understanding, nurturing and empathetic, these children can begin to feel less fear. It should be noted however that these vulnerable children often need some specialised help with the emotions, memories and internal coping mechanisms that are hardwired in their subconscious. Creative therapists can provide the unpacking and processing of these and that leads to behaviour changes and a transformed capacity for learning. In discussing the impact of a child feeling confused and unsafe regarding their relationships with adults, the impact is that the brain is then preoccupied with survival and therefore: 'A child who has an altered neurobiological emotional state, who is "wired" to be almost consistently ready for threat, is a child who struggles to engage in learning' (de Thierry 2015, p.32).

When a child has been traumatised

The impact on the child is on multiple levels of their life and yet with appropriate and skilled support, they can recover and the harm can be undone. There is more about the impact of trauma in my book *The Simple Guide to Child Trauma* (2016), including some activities to do with a child who has been traumatised to help them recover.

Some top tips to help them feel safe in a classroom or family setting:

- They will not naturally trust you as the adult to protect them or care for them and so don't assume using comforting words will be enough to reassure them!

- This feeling of distrust will often lead to them wanting to be in control or seeming to be defiant or overbearing. Or they will withdraw and be quiet or compliant. Give them jobs, ask them for their opinion, give them choices and pick your battles. If you are the parent, make sure that you have time set aside regularly to spend time one to one in a way that they look forward to, doing something you both enjoy.

- If they feel unsafe they will be easily triggered by things not going their way. Find out how they can feel safe when they are in distress, by trying out places and activities when they are in a calm space. Do they need instructions to be repeated or written down? Do they need to withdraw and go somewhere quiet if there is too much excitement? Do they need to be told about the order of events in enough time and space that they have time to ask questions? Do they have a space or a bag with comforting objects in it that they can quickly access? Do they have a way of telling you non-verbally that they feel scared? They could have a cushion, a sensory/fiddle bag, a special seat, a den or tent, a room to go to, etc. where they find pre-prepared things that they have chosen which bring them comfort and calm.

- If possible, find out any obvious triggers connected with their past trauma. Most triggers are complex sensory experiences that would be hard for them to know about, but some can easily be communicated, for example, the sound of an ambulance, being called dirty, feeling tummy pains of hunger, loud noises, etc. Then you can try and avoid them or respond quickly and calmly if they occur to help the child find calm and comfort with you.

- Aim to slowly build their trust by being repeatedly nurturing, kind, consistent, calm, caring and fun. It takes time, but is very rewarding.

Reflection points

- What behaviours are you familiar with from children with attachment difficulties?

- What have you found has helped a child with such difficulties form a relationship with you?

- What behaviours do you find the most triggering and challenging and what can you do to help stay regulated when those behaviours are displayed?

Chapter Eight

ATTACHMENT DIFFICULTIES

When a child has experienced fear and pain in the context of relationship, they can only experience healing in the context of relationships. For some children their experiences have led them to now struggle in significant ways. Ultimately:

1. They need several adults who can offer long term consistency, nurture, empathy and kindness. An adult who is not judgemental or punitive and where in the context of this relationship they get to experience co-regulation continually.

2. They need to be healed from the turmoil of not having their needs met in the early years by helping them process their feelings, memories and sadness which are locked up in their subconscious as a volcanic feeling. This requires trauma recovery focused creative psychotherapy.

Usually, by the time the adults around them have sought extra professional help, it has been evidenced strongly that the children are not able to work well with adults and instead demonstrate fear and uncertainty that leads them to take control so they feel less powerless.

It then takes the courage of one or two adults to offer the relationship the child needs despite their continual rejection and testing of it. This can be exhausting and frightening as the child continually tries to reject the adult before they can reject them and as they express pent up emotions that are strong and powerful and have the possibility of overwhelming both the child and the adult. As the adult(s) remain calm and non-rejecting, eventually the child is able to build new neural pathways of positive adult relationships that then consequently lead them to learn how to build other new relationships. The child's behaviour changes only as the positive adult(s) are able to be resilient and courageous enough to continue to show kindness in the face of the fear expression of the child that often displays itself as aggression and nastiness.

Sometimes a child has experienced terror from their primary attachment figure that has caused them to refuse to listen to or co-operate with adults unless they are in total control due to the levels of terror that are held in the subconscious. Anger and aggression are the clear external challenges that can require strategies for everyone to be kept safe, but actually there are often some complex subconscious coping mechanisms internally that need to be processed in a therapy context. These terrified children need caring, strong, kind, nurturing adults who can withstand the behaviours until the child is able to eventually believe the kindness and learn to trust. This is the route to healing, behaviour change and emotional regulation.

Rejection

The child can be so significantly traumatised by their experiences of adults that they will take years to develop a trust for those who are caring for them. The child can actively seek to stop the love and care that is being offered to them and harshly reject them instead. The child responds like that because they have often had experience of love that led to loss and so it seems easier and self protective to refuse to love or be loved. They often want to try and reject the adult before they get rejected and so therefore they can keep control of the relationship. Over time the behaviour that demonstrates rejection can be exhausting and deeply disheartening for the adult. When a parent feels that they are fighting to care for their child and that in response the child offers anger, hatred and rejection, it can be relentless and painful for the adult and can cause secondary trauma. The adult has to adopt coping mechanisms themselves to be able to cope with the rejection and so they often end up living with a heightened threat response where they are hypervigilant to the child's moods so that they can prepare for outbursts, aggressive tantrums and meltdowns. This then depletes the adult of emotional energy and can make it increasingly hard to care consistently for the child who is rejecting them. Whilst the adult usually understands some of the reasons for the child's behaviour and has deep empathy for their challenging early life experiences, it doesn't lessen the pain they feel themselves, as they have to focus on surviving their volatility and rejection.

Interaction with professionals

Sometimes when a child is in a cycle of rejecting the love and nurture offered, the situation can escalate when professional help is sought. The child can act differently with other adults which can make the parent or caring adult feel deeply frustrated because that can lead to them being told simple strategies which have often been used and the parent or caring adult is left feeling judged, misunderstood and that they have been seen as a failure. This puts further strain on the relationship between the traumatised child and the caring adult.

> We must remember that the visiting professional sees only the very tip of the 'challenging behaviour iceberg' whilst the carer has a wet suit on most of the time. (Naish 2016, p.29)

The key thing is for all the adults around the child to communicate well and the focus to be on supporting the caring adult emotionally as they do a life changing and highly demanding job of being consistent loving caregivers. Shaming, judging, blaming and not taking time to really understand the dynamics of a challenging relationship can increase the trauma for both parties. Empathy and respect can enable the adult to feel calm enough to reflect and be supported in the task and this can be achieved with time and understanding of the impact of attachment trauma.

Children recover from trauma in three ways

1. Through a consistent, kind, patient and caring relationship where repetitive relational interactions can change the neural pathways.

2. Through co-regulation with an adult who enables them to understand what different feelings are and tolerate them whilst also learning to express them constructively and know how to calm themselves in the face of fear and panic.

3. Through being able to process and make sense of the subconscious and body memories that are held as a consequence of the traumatic experience. This needs to be facilitated by those who understand how to keep the child safe whilst facilitating the processing – usually an experienced psychotherapist who uses creative methods.

It takes time and no short term intervention is likely to be successful. It's a long term commitment to seeing the neural pathways change and self regulation becoming a new healthy response to stress. These new skills enable the child to process the trauma and make sense of it, whilst beginning to trust and relax in the positive nurturing relationship with their caring adult.

Self care for the carer or parent of the child with attachment difficulties

It is vital that the parent or adult carer has time to focus on the vital self care that is needed to survive and thrive in the role of key nurturer. A few things to try and find:

1. Identifying good emotional support from friends and family who don't judge, shame, offer advice but make you food, tea and care for you.

2. A hobby or something that is relaxing for you. Time to process, breathe, relax and be an adult in your own right.

3. Enough sleep.

4. Making sure you remind each other that you can only try your best, you are doing brilliantly and

things change over time so celebrate each small shift...

Reflection points

- Do I know anyone with significant attachment trauma ?

- What can I do to offer an additional caring role model for them?

- What relationships enable you to feel calm and relaxed and cared for?

Chapter Nine

A HEALING ADULT RELATIONSHIP

I hope that this book has helped evidence the understanding that relationships are central to help a child with attachment difficulties heal and form a new internal expectation of others. Perry and Szalavitz explain that, 'the brain develops in a social context; one cannot develop a sense of self without a sense of the other' (2010, p.104).

When looking at the key qualities of an adult helping a child build strong and healthy attachments, Gerhardt found that responsiveness was the miracle ingredient. Once again, it's not as simple as it sounds and depends on a sense of intuition as all relationships do, but she says that:

> researchers have refined our knowledge to the point where we can now say that babies need not too much, not too little, but just the right amount of responsiveness – not the kind that jumps anxiously to meet their every need, nor the kind that ignores them for too long, but the kind of relaxed responsiveness that confident parents tend to have. (2004, p.197)

When an adult is available, responsive and nurturing in the first five years the internal structure is built for all future relationships and the child just needs to continue to be able to relate to a primary caregiver and other adults, expecting to be cared for. When a child hasn't had those early foundations put in place the way to build in the vital missing experiences is through repeated, regular and intentional relationships. It can be hard work providing the missing years of experience but also rewarding as you watch the child responding to the care, warmth and repeated positive relational experiences that can change the wiring of their brain.

Key character traits in an adult that enable healing

There are some key character traits that enable children to develop positive attachment relationships and therefore transform into having a positive 'internal working model' of relationships. When adults make themselves available to help rewire a child's brain and change their expectations of adults, they are changing their life forever. It's not always easy but it's exciting work if we hold the long term picture in view as we work with the day-to-day volatility and the child grapples with trying to assimilate their new positive information about relationships being potentially pleasurable.

The importance of consistency

Children who have experienced attachment relationships that have confused them, hurt them or not been available need to know that there are caring, available adults who can be consistent. Whilst we all have good days and days where we may struggle through, we need to still be consistent with the children in our care. They need us to be consistent in our care for them and to acknowledge that they need adults to help them. They need us to be consistently available and when we can't be to provide a reason and time to explain the reason. This consistency is the repetition that can rewire the brain's neural pathways to be able to trust others in a way that is positive and can facilitate healing.

Authenticity and saying sorry

As adults we are not always going to get it right and saying sorry in a way that is authentic rather than going through the motions can be really helpful for children. Healthy children are authentic and are not good at faking things. Their ability to be honest and transparent makes people know where they stand, which can be embarrassing but also helpful! When we as adults are authentic in being able to explain simply the things that are going on which the child may be worried about, with appropriate amounts of information and in a way that decreases anxiety and doesn't increase it, they feel that the relationship they are engaging in with us is an honest one where they are valued and part of it. Children can tell when we are faking it; it's better to be honest and say 'mummy is having a bad day today and everything seems to be making me grumpy. But it's definitely not your fault. Mummy needs to have a thinking space and work out what's going on. Is that OK? I'll try and be less grumpy in a few minutes...' Cozolino speaks of how important these relational elements are for the child to develop healthy hearts and minds: 'Somehow they have found a way to learn how to cognitively and emotionally process negative experiences with their parents, find others with whom to connect, and regulate their inner emotional worlds' (2006, p.325).

Playfulness and creativity

Playing is an essential activity to enable us all to process and make sense of life. It allows a sense of creativity and exploration that helps bring clarity and relaxation and also stimulation. It is the most important work for the child and it is an important part of living a balanced life as an adult. Winnicott, the great British psychoanalyst who gave us so many helpful theories, makes this profound statement: 'It is in playing and only in playing that the individual child or adult is able to be creative and to use the whole personality, and it is only in being creative that the individual discovers the self' (2005, p.73).

When we play with children and let them lead the process rather than dominate and control the play, we have the privilege of coming into their worlds and seeing things from their framework. We get to explore with them and learn from them. We are able to laugh and sigh and experience a range of emotions together with them. This play develops connection which in turn enables trust and a sense of being known by the other.

The process of facilitating the rewiring of neural pathways and healing the subconscious

Our aim in helping a child with attachment difficulties is to help rewire their brain where their subconscious is holding onto the belief that all adults are volatile and not to be trusted. Their mind may really want to trust you and be with you and probably they want you to love them and like them more than anything. The frustration is that their subconscious is often in conflict with their mind and they just can't seem to change it because it has so much control over their reactions, responses and feelings.

We sometimes explain this to the child by describing the brain in the two hemispheres, the left and right. We explain that everyone has a right and left side of the brain. The left side helps make sense of what the right brain picks up through sensory and non-verbal experience. The left brain processes what the right brain has experienced and tries to put it into words. If a child is struggling with overwhelming emotions or having done something that they don't understand, then they need an adult to help them make sense of what they are experiencing because their right brain is feeling overwhelmed. If the child is rejecting and running away from the adult, it's the right brain that is struggling to articulate what's going on in words and instead is acting from the survival, primitive brain. The child cannot quickly process the strong feelings or experiences that are overwhelming the right brain and they need the adult to help them. Ruby Wax says eloquently that we need:

> to tune into your kid's right brain, link up with them by using your own right brain, which picks up clues about their feelings through facial expressions, movements and tone of voice (specialties of the

right brain). This is called right to right attunement. Eighty per cent of all communication is done by those below the radar clues rather than speech. This right to right brain attunement is when the parent connects biologically with the child by mirroring emotions back to them, making them feel understood, Then, the parent can re direct the feelings from the child's right brain to their left (by using their own left brain) to help the child figure out a logical explanation and put feelings into words. When the right and left brain hook up, the feeling of helplessness and confusion passes and balance returns. (p.122)

Janie's story

We never expected to be grandparents parenting our grandchild full time! But things went so wrong for our son, we could see that it just wasn't best for Janie to stay with him. She was rude and angry, and when she lashed out it hurt even though she's only three. At nursery she was perfect – 'no fuss at all' they said – it was so frustrating. Then our parent support worker helped us to understand she was just communicating how unhappy, scared and muddled she was feeling inside with the people she felt safest with. She helped us to attune to Janie's needs and see what an impact it had if we consistently empathised with her rather than scolded her, and it's working! Janie doesn't 'melt down' nearly as much as she did and she's feeling more able to be herself at nursery too.

Holding a child in mind

This is a simple thing that helps build trust for the child who is struggling. The child may tell you about his collection of stones or his goldfish that is looking very still or his toe that hurts. Maybe our instinct is to sigh and comment that those things are hardly important or maybe our instinct is to say something like 'Aha, sure' and essentially ignore the comments. When we recognise the power of empathy and remember to 'step into his shoes' we realise that in his world these things are huge and so important. This shifts our reaction to being one with more feeling and an authentic interest. Then the most powerful thing is to remember the matter an hour or a day later and enquire about the stones, toe or goldfish! When we do this the child feels that we authentically care because we were thinking about him when he wasn't there and so we 'held him in mind' which means to them that we are doing more than fulfilling an obligation. The empathy from us as adults leading to holding the child in mind builds the relationship that can lead to the rewiring of neural pathways and thereby healing of the relational hurts in the past.

Finding professional help

With attachment disorders, attachment trauma and all trauma, it is worth trying to find a child or adol-escent psychotherapist who specialises in attachment and trauma. They can lead the sensitive task of helping the child process the subconscious and body memories and can add additional support to the complex reorganisation, rebuilding or healing of the primary attachment relationship.

A child, aged nine, after having therapy

This is how I feel now having been here with you helping me. First my head: I feel like I can express myself more. My shoulders: I don't scurry around thinking about bad things. My chest: I have learned to breathe better. My belly: my anger has gone down. When I am sad at school I can tell people a bit more. My legs: I have more energy because I can run around here. My arm: I feel like I express all my emotions more. I feel stronger in my arms. Now I don't hurt people and I know what to do. It's because you have been kind to me and helped me understand myself.

Reflection points

- What do you find the most natural approach to offer children – playfulness and creativity, authenticity and saying sorry, or consistency?

- What do you find the most challenging? Why do you think that is?

- Have you been helping a child who struggled to articulate their emotions or a traumatic experience but then became able to after a while?

Chapter Ten

RESILIENCE, BAD DAYS AND TOP TIPS!

We all know that investing into the lives of children is the most incredible privilege but also exhausting! We all have good days and bad days and we need help from each other. None of us can manage as professionals or parents or carers without the support of one another and we are all learning on the job! As new research comes out, it is incredible to see what some of us knew intuitively and what others of us had no idea of due to our backgrounds.

As we try our best here are a few ending tips to help us on our journey!

How much do the bad days impact the child?

I think parenting works similar to an Amazon book review! You know that most of the time people who appreciate the book don't say anything and there's a mixed response from the times when people do say! There is then an average of the responses that people pop on to the website. As a parent, carer or professional, I think we need to recognise that most of the time when we are doing a great job we won't be told or affirmed and when we do get feedback it may not be reflective of the reality of the overall response! So I think we can work on our overall average response and be comfortable if we are averaging more good responses than negative and always take in the context of the negative responses! I am a full believer in children growing up understanding that we grown ups have grumpy days, sad days and bad days and I always explain that to the children I am around and then watch to make sure that they don't feel responsible and don't feel anxious. If they do, then I use that as a great time to focus on helping them process their reactions and thus they become emotionally literate and healthy! If I had been always happy then I'm not sure my ability to model emotional processing would be such a helpful resource to enable my own children to be comfortable and articulate about their own range of emotions.

How can we help them with friendships?

I think that watching our children navigate their relationships can be difficult, especially if we didn't have an easy time of friendships as children. I think the role we have is one of emotional co-regulation, being a safe place to help them make sense of their world and feel comforted and supported, give them some tips and insight and then trust them to navigate their way through all the intricacies that we are not around to see. It's important to stay attuned and check in on how things are and respond appropriately but within the boundaries that they need to go on the journey with our support and not detailed direction at every turn.

If we help them process, make sense and explore their emotions, reactions and responses then they will in turn develop healthy relationships, that will go on to become a lifelong skill. Bomber points out that friendships follow a secure relationship with an adult:

> We need to be actively involved in providing appropriate structure for children with attachment difficulties to make and keep friends. We mustn't assume that they are developmentally ready for independence. Remember that need to have experienced a strong relationship with a consistent, sensitive adult prior to negotiating independence. (Bomber 2007, p.222)

Other top tips to build positive relationships with children

Physical contact

Children need physical contact. As parents and carers we need to explore what they feel comfortable with and always enable them to have power to say 'not now' and 'I need space' and other indications that they don't want physical touch. Their bodies do belong to them and as such they shouldn't ever be expected to offer physical contact to adults due to feeling manipulated, expected, demanded or required. They need to be empowered to make choices about hugs, stroking and kisses and always have the ability to say no. Boundaries are important but also a recognition that natural touches such as warm hugs are important for them to feel safe and secure, unless they have been hurt in this way in which case they will need more space and time to work out what they need. It is equally important to navigate the need for some children to spend time alone reflecting or creating and yet for others that would feel like abandonment. This exploration of each child's needs can be exhausting and volatile but is essential to be able to facilitate what they need.

Being fun, having fun and making memories

To invest in any attachment relationship we need to take time to enjoy ourselves, have fun and make memories. Having a meal, playing a game and days out all help build relationships. For children with attachment difficulties, the short, regular, fun activities slowly rebuild their ability to enjoy them without being emotionally deregulated. Cozolino describes here how we can remind ourselves the important work that we are doing when we invest our time and energy into children who have experienced negative attachment experiences: 'Adults who thrive despite childhood neglect and abuse often describe life affirming experiences with others who made them feel cared for and worthwhile. The potential for healing relationships is all around us' (2006, p.314).

Listening so they feel heard

When we listen so that others feel heard, it changes that relationship. Think of a time when you were speaking with someone who either had negative body language, was emotionally not present or was distracted and kept checking their phone or the clock. How did you feel? Did it make you want to open out and talk more or did you cut the conversation short or lose your train of thought? Children pick up how interested we are in what they have to say and the problem is that the biggest worry in their world could seem so daft compared to our worries that we could feel cross or irritated, unless we remember that, in their world, their worry is a big deal. It's hard to show that we value their concern about if they are having sausages for tea and if their plate is yellow when our worries could be about paying bills or resolving important relational conflicts, but when we put ourselves in their shoes, our response can then calm, reassure and help them rather than disconnect them and frustrate them. They then feel heard and valued and so trust builds in the relationship.

Charlie's story

My parent worker has taught me how to 'clean up my mess'. If I get it wrong and I do accidently dismiss Charlie when he needs to talk to me or even shout at him, I go to him and tell him it was wrong of mummy to shout and that I am very sorry. I ask him to forgive me. I know I've just role modelled to him what to do if he makes a mistake and how we can always 'wipe the slate clean' and start over again. It helps me remember he wants things to be forgiven and not remembered too.

Containment, transference and countertransference

These three words can help us understand some of the complexities of relationships. Containment is a helpful word that can describe some of what we have to do as the adult in an attachment relationship. We offer the child the necessary privilege of pouring out their confusion, pain, upset and worries onto us and we 'contain' it all. We can't always fix the situations but we can 'contain' the emotions for them by listening, emotionally connecting and validating their feelings rather than dismissing them. The containing process starts in babyhood as the baby projects the unmanageable feelings onto the primary caregiver, who in turn reflects them back such that they become more tolerable for the infant.

It can be tough work being the 'container' sometimes, especially when we feel full of our own 'stuff' and that's why we need to encourage each other and offer support to each other when the kids in our world need us to 'contain' a lot of negative feelings and muddles.

Transference is a psychological concept that was first described by Freud in 1895 as a word that describes the experience of a person subconsciously (unintentionally) transferring their feelings and thoughts about someone else to you as you connect with them. This can be confusing as they are not aware that they are doing it, but the reactions and responses that the person has are more appropriate to another person in their life rather than you! As someone over 40 years old, I often have this experience as people project their feelings about their mother or childhood headteacher onto me without knowing it and I ponder on how they have made so many judgements about me! Countertransference is the reaction we can have when someone does that, which is a reaction to their transference or projection. In the case of someone subconsciously reacting to me as if I was a headteacher, countertransference would be taking on that headteacher role and feeling like I had that position even when I didn't. It's all subconscious and is a deep layer of reactions that we often don't fully understand as they can surprise us! Some children will respond to us as if we are an original attachment figure who hurt them even though they know we aren't like them at all.

Core beliefs

Many children who have struggled with attachment experiences grow up with negative core beliefs about themselves and the world. They can carry around feelings of shame, worthlessness, rejection and loneliness which are often accompanied by beliefs such as 'I'm useless'; 'No one really wants to know me'; 'If you come close to me you'll soon reject me anyway so I may as well reject you now to save us all disappointment'; 'I don't belong anywhere and I don't fit in'. These negative core beliefs can be so deeply enmeshed in their thinking and behaviour that it takes a long time of consistent, repetitive, kind, patient, nurturing and forgiving relationship to enable them to slowly break the hold on their minds. Eventually, when they have enough experiences of kindness, nurture and care, alongside some work 'spotting them' and bringing these negative thoughts from the subconscious to the conscious, they lose their power and can be replaced with positive ones.

We aim for children to grow up learning and experiencing the following positive and healthy beliefs:

- I am wanted and loved.

- If I was not around people would miss me.

- I have unique gifts and skills and I want to use them!

- I belong to a group who value me.

- I have a few special people who adore me.

- I am enjoying learning more about myself.

- Although I'm not perfect and I make mistakes, I am loved.

- I can let people know if I have needs and they will help me.

- I am loveable.

- I am safe.

- I am helpful, friendly and kind.

- I am generous, loving and brave.

Children learn these things, not from what we say to them, but from how we say it to them and how we then behave around them! As they begin to experience more and more positive relational experiences the core beliefs slowly change and their confidence and sense of self identity increases.

Conclusion

Our aim as adults is not to be perfect, but to be authentic, caring and quick to repair any mistakes we make. We can develop strong attachments for the very young by our intentional care and knowledge of their developmental needs. For those children and young people who have experienced attachment difficulties and trauma, we can be the ones to invest in their repair before they carry the pain into adulthood. It's not always easy, but it is always worthwhile taking the time and skill to attune, listen, care, play, be creative and emotionally connect with those in our care. We really are changing lives!

REFERENCES

Ainsworth, M.D.S., Blehar, M.C., Waters, E. and Wall, S. (1978) *Patterns of Attachment: A Psychological Study of the Strange Situation.* Hillsdale, NJ: Erlbaum.

Benoit, D. (2018) 'Infant-parent attachment: Definition, types, antecedents, measurement and outcome.' *Pediatric Child Health 9,* 8, 541–545.

Bomber, L.M. (2007) *Inside I'm Hurting. Practical Strategies for Supporting Children with Attachment Difficulties in Schools.* London: Worth Publishing.

Bowlby, J. (1988) *A Secure Base.* New York, NY: Basic Books.

Casey, P. and Strain, J. (2016) *Trauma and Stressor Related Disorders: A Handbook for Clinicians Paperback.* Philadelphia, PA: American Psychiatric Publishing.

Cozolino, L. (2006) *The Neuroscience of Human Relationships. Attachment and the Developing Social Brain.* New York, NY: W.W. Norton and Company.

Crittenden, P. (2005) 'Attachment theory, psychopathology, and psychotherapy: The dynamic-maturational approach. ['Teoria dell'attaccamento, psicopatologia e psicoterapia: L'approccio dinamico maturativo.']' *Psicoterapia 30,* 171–182.

Cyr, C., Euser, E.M., Bakermans-Kranenburg, M.J and Van Ijzendoorn, M.H. (2010) 'Attachment security and disorganisation in maltreating and high risk families: A series of meta–analyses.' *Development and Psychopathology 22,* 1, 87–108.

de Thierry, B. (2015) *Teaching the Child on the Trauma Continuum.* London: Grosvenor Publishing.

de Thierry, B. (2016) *The Simple Guide to Child Trauma.* London: Jessica Kingsley Publishers.

de Thierry, B. (2018) *The Simple Guide to Understanding Shame in Children*. London: Jessica Kingsley Publishers.

Fonagy P., Gergely G., Jurist E. L. and Target M. (2002) *Affect Regulation, Mentalization, and the Development of the Self*. New York, NY: Other Press.

Gerhardt, S. (2004) *Why Love Matters. How Affection Shapes a Baby's Brain*. Hove: Brunner-Routledge.

Howes, C. (1999) 'Attachment Relationships in the Context of Multiple Caregivers.' In J. Cassidy and P.R. Shaver (eds) *Handbook of Attachment: Theory, Research, and Clinical Applications*. New York, NY: Guilford Press.

Klaus, M.H. and Kennell, J.H. (1976) *Maternal-Infant Bonding: The Impact of Early Separation or Loss on Family Development*. St Louis, MO: Mosby.

Levine, P. and Kline, M. (2006) *Trauma through a Child's Eyes. Awakening the Ordinary Miracle of Healing*. Berkeley, CA: North Atlantic Books.

Naish, S. (2016) *Therapeutic Parenting in a Nutshell Positives and Pitfalls*. CreateSpace Independent Publishing Platform.

Pearce, C. (2009) *A Short Introduction to Attachment and Attachment Disorder*. London: Jessica Kingsley Publishers.

Perry, B. and Szalavitz, M. (2010) *Born for Love. Why Empathy Is Essential and Endangered*. New York, NY: HarperCollins.

Perry, N.B., Dollar, J.M., Calkins, S.D., Keane, S.P. and Shanahan, L. (2018) 'Childhood self-regulation as a mechanism through which early overcontrolling parenting is associated with adjustment in preadolescence.' *Developmental Psychology 54*, 8, 1542–1554.

Reisz, S., Duschinsky, R. and Siegel, D.J. (2017) 'Disorganized attachment and defense: Exploring John Bowlby's unpublished reflections.' *Attachment & Human Development*. DOI: 10.1080/14616734.2017.1380055.

Sameroff, A. (2010) 'A unified theory of development: A dialectic integration of nature and nurture.' *Child Development 81*, 6–22.

Schaffer, H.R. and Emerson, P.E. (1964) 'The development of social attachments in infancy.' *Monographs of the Society for Research in Child Development*, 1–77.

Shemmings, D. (2016a) 'A quick guide to attachment theory.' *The Guardian*, 15 February. Available at www.theguardian.com/social-care-network/2016/feb/15/attachment-theory-social-work-child-protection, accessed on 12 May, 2017.

Shemmings, D. (2016b) 'Making sense of disorganised attachment behaviour in pre-school children.' *International Journal of Birth and Parent Education 4*, 1, 21–26.

Siegel, D. (2001) 'Toward an interpersonal neurobiology of the developing mind: Attachment, relationships, mindsight and neural integration.' *Infant Mental Health Journal 22*, 1–2, 67–94. Available at www.communityofmindfulparenting.com/curriculum/week2/S2-Article-FiveBasictoFosterSecureAttachment.pdf, accessed on 12 May, 2017.

Siegel, D. (2011) *The Whole Brain Child. Revolutionary Strategies to Nurture Your Child's Developing Mind*. New York, NY: Delacorte Press.

Sullivan, R., Perry, R., Sloan, A., Kleinhaus, K. and Burtchen, N. (2011) 'Infant bonding and attachment to the caregiver: Insights from basic and clinical science.' *Clinics in Perinatology 38*, 4, 643–655.

Wax, R. (2018) *Ruby Wax with a Neuroscientist and a Monk, How to Be Human: The Manual*. London: Penguin Life.

Winnicott, D.W. (1960) 'The theory of parent-infant relationship.' *International Journal of Psycho-analysis 41*, 585–595.

Winnicott, D.W. (2005) *Playing and Reality*. Oxford: Routledge.

World Health Organization (2018) *International Standard Classification of Diseases and Related Health Problems, ICD-11*. Geneva: WHO.

FURTHER READING

Association for Psychological Science (2011) 'Can fetus sense mother's psychological state? Study suggests yes.' *Science Daily*, 10 November. Available at www.sciencedaily.com/ releases/2011/11/111110142352.htm, accessed on 15 November, 2018.

Erksine, R.G. (1998) 'Attunement and involvement: Therapeutic responses to relational needs.' *International Journal of Psychotherapy 3*, 3.

Kinsella, M.T. and Monk, C. (2009) 'Impact of maternal stress, depression and anxiety on fetal neurobehavioral development.' *Clinical Obstetrics and Gynecology 52*, 3, 425–440.

Weiland, S. (2011) *Dissociation in Traumatised Children and Adolescents*. New York, NY: Routledge.

INDEX